Robert Bowes

Biographical Notes on the University Printers from the

Commencement of Printing in Cambridge to the Present

Time

Robert Bowes

Biographical Notes on the University Printers from the Commencement of Printing in Cambridge to the Present Time

ISBN/EAN: 9783337254926

Printed in Europe, USA, Canada, Australia, Japan

Cover: Foto ©ninafisch / pixelio.de

More available books at **www.hansebooks.com**

BIOGRAPHICAL NOTES ON THE UNIVERSITY PRINTERS FROM THE COMMENCEMENT OF PRINTING IN CAMBRIDGE TO THE PRESENT TIME. BY ROBERT BOWES.

Reprinted for private circulation from the *Cambridge Antiquarian Society's Communications*, No. XXVI. (Vol. v. No. 4) 1886.

CONTENTS.

XX. Biographical Notes on the University Printers from the Commencement of Printing in Cambridge to the Present Time. Communicated by Robert Bowes, Esq.

[January 28, 1884.]

Introductory.

The following pages are the result of an attempt to trace the succession of University printers and to ascertain how far and for how long each printer was actually engaged in the management of the Press. Many of the printers appointed before 1700 appear never to have been so engaged. These were for the most part graduate members of the University holding other offices (Esquire Bedell, Registrary, etc.) and received a small salary. The smallness of this salary (£5 a year, occasionally increased by a gratuity of the same amount) makes it seem probable that the office was looked upon as a sinecure, and that an appointment was made when a vacancy occurred in order to preserve the right of the University to appoint three printers. The printers of the latter class certainly held their office on a different footing, as, for instance, John Hayes was paying £100 a year to the University at the same time that Hugh Martin and Jonathan Pindar were receiving £5 a year from the University.

My information has been mainly obtained from well-known authorities, such as:

Ames, *Typographical Antiquities*, 1749; and the second edition by Herbert, 3 vols., 1785–1790 (cited as Ames-Herbert).

Carter, *Hist. of the University of Cambridge*, 1753 (taken almost entirely from the first edition of Ames).

Nichols, *Literary Anecdotes and Literary Illustrations*, 17 vols., 1812–1858.

Watt, *Bibliotheca Britannica*, 4 vols., 1824.

Cooper, *Annals of Cambridge*, 4 vols., 1841–1852, and later writers. But beside these I have had the advantage of consulting certain sources of evidence, some of which are not so generally accessible, viz :

1. Documents in the Registry.

2. A Chronological List (MS.) of all documents, entries in the Grace-books, and other material in the Registry relating to the Press, compiled by Mr A. P. Humphry.

3. The Minute-Book of the Curators of the Press, 1696–1740.

4. The Registers of the Stationers' Company from 1554 to 1640, edited by Edward Arber.

5. The Churchwardens' Books of St Mary the Great, 1583–1630.

6. The Churchwardens' Books of St Edward's, 1625—1670.

7. The Churchwardens' Books and Rate-Books, etc., of St Botolph's, 1646–1743, and Registers of Baptisms, Deaths, etc., 1617–1743.

8. The *Additions* to Cooper's *Annals of Cambridge*. These sheets were never published. They were discovered in a grocer's shop, where they were being used as waste-paper, when only three copies could be made up. Of these three copies one is in the University Library, one in the Cambridge Free Library, and the third is in my possession. The sheets are

marked Vol. v. Q Ff, pp. 225-448. Of Vol. v. only one part, pp. 1—128, has been published.

Besides eliciting a small amount of new matter, I have been enabled by consulting the above original sources to verify some statements which had appeared previously and to correct others.

Since the paper was read before the Society, I have received from friends many additions and corrections; and I am especially indebted to Mr F. Jenkinson, not only for the footnotes signed J., but for material help and advice on the paper as a whole. I shall still feel grateful to any one who will point out any inaccuracies that he may discover.

For access to the MS. matter my thanks are due to Dr Luard, Mr J. W. Clark, Mr A. P. Humphry, Mr C. J. Clay, Dr Campion, and the churchwardens of the several parishes named.

It will be convenient, as a preliminary step, to exhibit in a tabular form the chronological order of the printers, as far as I have been able to ascertain it, with the dates of their appointment.

CHRONOLOGICAL LIST OF UNIVERSITY PRINTERS.

(In the following list the names of those who are not known to have printed anything are in italics.)

1521.	John Siberch.	He disappears after 1522.
1534.	*Nicholas Speryng.*	
	Garratt Godfrey.	
	Sygar Nicholson.	
1539.	*Nicholas Pilgrim.*	
1540.	*Richard Noke.*	
1545.	*Peter Sheres.*	
1577.	*John Kingston.*	
1583.	Thomas Thomas, M.A.	d. 1588.
1588.	John Legate.	d. 1620.
?	*John Porter* (before 1593).	
1606.	Cantrell Legge.	He did not print after 1625.
?	*Thomas Brooke, M.A.* (before 1614). At least till 1621.	

1622.	Leonard Greene.	d. 1630.
1625.	Thomas Buck, M.A.	Said to have resigned 1653.
	John Buck. M.A.	(?)
1630.	Francis Buck.	Resigned 1632.
1632.	Roger Daniel.	Patent cancelled 1650.
1650.	John Legate (the younger).	Patent cancelled 1655.
1655.	John Field.	d. 1668.
1669.	*Matthew Whinn.*	
1669.	John Hayes.	d. 1705.
1680.	*John Peck, M.A.*	
1682.	*Hugh Martin, M.A.*	
1683.	*Dr James Jackson.*	
1683.	*Jonathan Pindar.*	
1693.	*H. Jenkes.*	
1697.	*Jonathan Pindar.*	At least till 1730.
1701.	John Owen.	Bankrupt 1703.
1705.	Cornelius Crownfield.	Pensioned 1740.

1730.	W. Fenner ⎫	
	Mrs Fenner ⎬ Lease relinquished by Mrs Fenner 1738.	
	Thomas James ⎭	
	John James	
1740.	Joseph Bentham.	Resigned 1766.
1758.	John Baskerville.	Nothing after 1763.
1766.	John Archdeacon.	Died 1795.
1793.	John Burges.	Died 1802.
1802.	John Deighton.	Resigned 1802.
1802.	Richard Watts.	Resigned 1809.
1804.	Andrew Wilson.	(?) 1811.
1809.	John Smith.	Pensioned 1836.
1836.	John William Parker.	Resigned 1853.

1854.	Charles John Clay.	
	George Seeley.	Retired 1856.
1882.	John Clay.	

1. JOHN SIBERCH.

John Siberch printed several books at Cambridge in the
years 1521 and 1522; and although he was not, strictly
speaking, a University printer, he naturally finds a place here
as being in a certain sense the precursor of the University

printers. An entry in Dr Caius's *Annales*[1] under date 1569 informs us that Siberch occupied a house between the Gate of Humility and the Gate of Virtue under the sign of the *Arma Regia*. This statement is most interesting, as, besides marking the exact spot on which our first printer worked, it explains how the arms of France and England quarterly came to be used as a device in some of Siberch's books[2].

Erasmus writing[3] on Christmas-day, 1525, to Dr Robert Aldrich of King's College, afterwards Bishop of Carlisle, sends greetings to "veteres sodales Phaunum, Omfridum, Vachanum, "Gerardum, Nicolaum, et Joannem Siburgum bibliopolas." Unless Erasmus had had no information about Siberch for some years, this would seem to imply that the latter was still in Cambridge in the year 1525.

Beyond this I have seen nothing that gives any information about Siberch; where he came from when he commenced printing in Cambridge in 1521, or what became of him after 1522. I should rejoice if the statement of this fact might lead some one with the necessary time and interest in the subject to try and supply these particulars.

The list of his books as found in the published bibliographies has grown up gradually. For two we are indebted to Maittaire in 1722; for three more to Palmer in 1732; Ames in 1749 raised the number to seven, and an eighth was added by Herbert in 1790. Since that date no fresh book from his press has been discovered. Ames suspected that there was a second book printed in 1522, having seen the last leaf of a book ending "Impressum in Alma Cantabrigia per me "Joannem Siberch, anno Domini MDXXII 8 Decembris." But further investigation has not confirmed this suspicion. As the

[1] For this information I am indebted to Mr Bensly, Librarian of Caius College.
[2] See Appendix A.
[3] *Opera* (Lugd. Bat. 1703), vol. III. pars. 1. col. 901 (epist. 782).

result of enquiries made for copies of books printed by Siberch, a copy of *Papyrius Geminus*, the eighth book in Herbert's list, was discovered in St John's College Library and brought to my notice by Dr Wood. The last leaf proved to contain the imprint quoted above, and it became evident that Ames was in fact describing a detached leaf of this book, of which he had apparently never seen a perfect copy.

In a volume in the same library containing two of the eight known books Thomas Baker has written these notes:

Erasmus *de conscribendis epistolis* and Henry Bullock's *Oration to Cardinal Wolsey* etc. are two of the first books, that I (or Mr Bagford who has seen more books than most men in England) ever saw, printed at Cambridge. One other book I have seen printed the same year [1521] and no more.

Dr Fuller [*Hist: of Cambr*: P: 58, 59.] seems to be of the same opinion, tho' he had never seen Erasmus his book, as appears by mistakes there made.

I never could meet with another copy of either of these books in this University.

I have since seen one in C. C. C. of Erasmus.

Besides these two books, I have only seen one other printed by Siberch at Cambridge this year viz: an: 1521, and there he styles himself, *Joannes Siberch primus utriusque* linguae in Angliâ impressor.

T. B.

In Hearne's *Walter Hemyngforde* (p. 735) there is a somewhat similar note taken from a copy of Erasmus given to Hearne by Baker.

I have not entered into any details respecting the books printed by Siberch, as an examination of the eight books has been made by Mr Bradshaw, and his notes will appear in a reproduction of Bullock's *Oration*.

2. NICHOLAS SPERYNG.
3. GARRETT GODFREY.
4. SEGAR NICHOLSON.

This appointment was made by Grace of the Senate, under the power granted by letters patent of the king, July 20, 1534, "to assign and elect from time to time by writing under the "seal of the Chancellor of the University three stationers and "printers or sellers of books, residing within the University," etc.[1] They were to print or import for sale only books approved by the censors of the University. This was in accordance with a petition which had been presented to Wolsey by the University in 1529.

The terms of the Grace, which occurs last but one among the Graces from Mich. 1533 to Mich. 1534 (Grace Book Γ. 148), are as follows:

Yt ys grawntyd that the vnyuersyte shall assine & chose accordyngo to your grauute lately made & geven yow by the Kyngs grace at the procuratyon and costis of Nycholas Sperynge, Garret Godfrey, & Segar Nycolsun the same forsayde three Statyoners to have & ynioy all & synguler lybertyes & priuylegis specyfyed yn the same graunte for terme of ther naturall lyvys, so that thei shall fullfyll at all tymes all & synguler dewtys mencyoned yn the same graunte belongyng to them on ther party, and that thei may have this your assygnatyon & eloctyon of them yn wrytyngis sygnd wythe yowre common scale.

Speryng, Godfrey and Nicholson were all in business in Cambridge before their appointment as printers and stationers to the University; and although there is no reason to suppose that they ever printed anything, we can still point to books which are almost undoubtedly specimens of their work as binders[2].

Godfrey lived in St Mary's parish, and appears as one of the

[1] Cooper's *Annals*, vol. I. p. 368.
[2] See Appendix A.

Churchwardens in 1517; and in the Parish Book for the year 31 Hen. VIII. (1539) there are the following entries:

> Item for the buryall of Garrett Godfreye vi' viij^d.
>
> *   *   *
>
> Item for the dyrge of Garrett Godfraye ij'.

and in the following years we still find

> Item for Garrett Godfreys Dyrgo vi^d.

It has been suggested[1] that Garrett Godfrey may be the same as Gerard the friend and bookseller of Erasmus, and "Garret our bookbynder" whom Ascham[2] mentions as well acquainted with the habits of Erasmus.

Speryng also lived in St Mary's parish, and appears as Churchwarden in 1516.

Nicholson was a member of Gonville Hall[3]; and it is remarkable, in view of his present appointment, that so lately as 1529 he had been accused of "holding Lutheran opinions "and having in his house the works of Luther and other pro- "hibited books without presenting them to the Ordinary[4]." In

---

[1] By Mr Searle in his *History of Queens' College*, p. 155, where (besides the letter written from Basle on Christmas Day, 1525, already mentioned, p. 287) he quotes *Opera*, vol. III. col. 130 (Epist. 148) salutabis... veterem hospitem meum Gerardum; col. 121-2 (Epist. 141) bibliopolam.

Mr Searle also quotes (*ib.* pp. 188, 189) two entries from the account books of Queens' College.

[1529.] Item Cegarto bibliopolle [Sygar Nicholson] pro constructione duorum illorum librorum in quibus statuta nostra conscribuntur cum reliquo corundem ornatu et pro stapo papyri regii qui in eorum altero constringitur   iiij s. iiij d.

[1531.] Item 2° die Maji Gerardo [Goodfrey] bibliopola (*sic*) pro libro in quem statuta transcribuntur   viij d.

[2] *Toxophilus* (ed. Arber), p. 46.

[3] Some interesting remarks upon the frequency with which members of the University in those days were engaged as tradesmen in the town, will be found in Mr Mullinger's *University of Cambridge to* 1535, p. 627.

[4] Cooper's *Annals*, I 329. He quotes Baker MSS. XXIV. 82; "the following charges in the accounts of John Lyndesey and Thomas Wilson.

fact it seems to have been in connexion with this prosecution that the University applied to Wolsey for leave to appoint stationers who should be under their own control.

The names of Nicholson or Segar occur three times in Arber's *Registers of the Stationers' Company.*

1557. Fraunces Nycholson *alias* Seager (I. 69).

1565. Benjamen Nycholas *alias* Seger of Chambryge apprenticed (I. 285).

1595. Beniamyn Segar *alias* Nycolson receives an apprentice (II. 207).

5. NICHOLAS PILGRIM.

The Grace for his appointment as Printer is dated 16 October 1539, from which it would appear that he was appointed to fill the vacancy caused by the death of Garrett Godfrey.

6. RICHARD NOKE.

A Grace for sealing his Patent occurs in 1540.

7. PETER SHERES.

The Grace for his appointment as Stationer or Printer is dated 5 February 154⅗.

8. JOHN KINGSTON.

The Grace for appointment of John Kingston is dated 8 February 157⅖, and a copy of the Patent is in Grace-book

Proctors, appear to refer to this matter : 'To Edw. Heynes on account of his office as scribe in the proceedings against Sygar for Heresy, 8s.': 'To the minister of the University for keeping of the same Sygar in prison during the time of his examination, 3s. 4d.': 'For faggots for burning books, 4d.'"

Δ, 282 a. On 18 July 1577, Lord Burghley wrote to Dr Goad, Vice-Chancellor, on the subject of Kingston's appointment, and disapproved of printing Psalters, Prayer Books, &c., as interfering with the Queen's grants to Seres, Jugge, Day, and others[1]. Notwithstanding the grant of the patent, Kingston seems never to have printed in Cambridge.

9. THOMAS THOMAS.

Thomas Thomas, born in London 25 December 1553, was educated at Eton and at King's College, Cambridge, where he became a Fellow in 1574. He was appointed University Printer by Grace 3 May 1583. He at once began to print a book by William Whitaker, but the Company of Stationers seized his press and materials. This seizure is spoken of in a letter, 1 June 1583, from the Bishop of London to Lord Burghley: "There was alsoe found one presse and furniture " which is saide to belonge to one Thomas a man (as I heare) " vtterlie ignorauntc in printinge, and pretendinge that he en- "tendeth to be the printer for the vniuersitie of Cambridge[2]." On June 14 of the same year the Vice-Chancellor and Heads, in reply to a letter from Lord Burghley suggesting a Conference with the Company of Stationers, urge the speedy return of Thomas's press that the Stationers had seized, and express the willingness of the University to confer with the Stationers. On the 16th of March, 1584, Lord Burghley replied to a further letter from the University, stating that he had submitted their Charter to the Master of the Rolls, who concurred with him in the opinion that it was valid[3]. On the 24th of July, 1584, Thomas Thomas, M.A. and printer, entered into

[1] Baker MSS. XXIX. 374, quoted in Cooper's *Annals*, II. 357.
[2] Arber, *Stat. Reg.* I. 246.
[3] Cooper, *Ann.* II. 393.

recognizances in 500 marks before the Vice-Chancellor, subject to the following condition :

If the said Tho. Thomas do not or shall not print or cause to be printed any book, pamphlet, or paper after he hath once finished Saddils werks[1], which he hath now under his press, until further order shall be taken with him by the Rt Hon. the Lord Treasurer our Chancellor, Mr Vice-Chancellor, and the University, that then this recognizance to be void and of none effect, or else to stand in full strength[2].

In 1584 books began to issue from Thomas's press, and Herbert gives the titles of 17 that appeared between that year and 1588. He was at the same time engaged on his Latin Dictionary, which bears the date in the dedication of September 1587; and the great labour of this work is said to have brought on a grievous disease which shortened his life. He died 9 August 1588, and was buried in Great St Mary's Church[3].

His attainments as a scholar and a printer combined are spoken of with admiration by his successor John Legate, in the dedication to Lord Chancellor Bacon of the 11th edition of the Latin Dictionary, published in 1619;

He was about 30 years ago a famous Printer among your Cantabrigians; yes something more than a Printer such as we now are, who understand the Latin that we print no more than Bellerophon the letters he carried, and who sell in our shops nothing of our own except the paper *black with the press's sweat*[4]. But he, a companion of the Stephenses and of the other, very few, printers of the true kind and best omen, was of opinion that it was men of learning, thoroughly imbued with academic studies, who should give themselves to cultivating and rightly applying that illustrious benefit sent down from heaven and given to aid mankind and perpetuate the

[1] *Sudeclis Disputationes Theologicae et Scholasticae* published by Thomas in 1584, 4to.
[2] Baker MSS. III. 430, quoted by Cooper (*Additions to Annals*, p. 289), who also refers [*ib.* 301] to a letter, dated July 27, 1588, from the Bishop of Lincoln to Lord Burghley on behalf of Thomas, in MS. Baker, vi. 293; MS. Lansd. lvii., Art. 74; Heywood and Wright, *Univ. Trans.* i. 534.
[3] Cooper, *Ath. Cant.* II. 29, 543.
[4] ' preli sudore nigrantem'.

arts. Accordingly what more fit than that when he had wrought what was worthy of type, he should himself, needing aid of none, act as midwife to his own progeny.

Thomas's printing-office, according to Leonard Greene writing about 1629[1], was in the Regent Walk, which was immediately opposite the west door of St Mary's Church.

I can find only two entries in the Parish Book that refer to Thomas. In the Churchwardens' accounts for 1584 he appears as paying 6s. 8d. rate; and in 1589 Mrs Thomas pays " for the buriall of her husband 6s. 8d."

10. JOHN LEGATE.

John Legate, the immediate successor of Thomas, was appointed by Grace, 2 November 1588, "as he is reported to be skilful in the art of printing books." He was the first who used (from 1603 onward) the impression of the *Alma Mater Cantabrigiæ* with the motto *Hinc lucem et pocula sacra* round it, and he seems to have printed at Cambridge till about 1609. He is stated by Carter to have resigned in 1607; but while after 1609(?) all books with his name have *London* on the title-page, he still continues to call himself 'Printer to the University' and to use the University design. His right to this title is confirmed by an entry in a MS. account of the University written by John Scot, Notary Public, in 1617, where his name appears, with those of 'Canterell Legg' and Thomas Brooke, as one of the three University printers.

In the Registers of the Company of Stationers (Arber IV. 45), there is an entry by John Legate (the younger), 21 August 1620, of certain books "the copies of John Legat his father lately deceased," so that we may take 1620 to be the year of his death,

[1] Registry MS. 33. 1. 11. The passage is quoted below in my notes on Thomas Buck (p. 300,.

and not 1626 as stated by Ames and subsequent writers[1]. He was admitted and sworn a Freeman of the Stationers' Company in April, 1586[2], and was Master of the Company in 1604[3]. He married Agatha, daughter of Christopher Barker, the King's printer, and left 11 children, his son John succeeding him[4].

In 1612, an edition of Perkins's Works is described as to be sold at his house in Trinitie Lane. This, Mr Henry B. Wheatley informs me, was called after the Church of the Holy Trinity, which was destroyed in the Great Fire and not rebuilt, and is described as between Old Fish Street and Bow Lane.

Under date 1 August 1597, the following entry appears in the Stationers' Registers[5], showing that at that date Legate was recognized by the Stationers as University printer:

WHEREAS John legat hathe printed at Cambridge by Aucthoritie of the vniuersitie there a booke called the *Reformed Catholike:* This seid booke is here Registred for his copie so that none of this Company shall prynt yt from hym. PROVIDED that this entrance shalbe voyd yf the seid booke be not Aucthorised by the seid vniuersitie as he saieth it is, vj[d].

He had a grant of the exclusive right of printing for a term of years Thomas's *Dictionary*, as augmented by him [Legate]; and the 11th edition, from the dedication of which an extract has been made under Thomas Thomas (see p. 293), appeared in 1619, the year before his death. This right was renewed to John Legate, his son, on behalf of himself and 10 others his brothers and sisters, 11 February 162$\frac{0}{1}$[6].

Legate's name appears in the St Mary's Parish Book from 1590 to 1610: from 1591 to 1609 there is an annual entry "For "Rent of hys shopp 5s.", and in 1610, "Received of Mr Williams

---

[1] It is a further confirmation of this that in John Scot's *Foundation of the University* written in 1621 (British Museum, Add. MSS. 11720), Legge and Brooke are given as printers, while the third place is left blank.

[2] Arber II. 696.   [3] Arber II. 737.

[4] Ames *Typographical Antiquities*, page 462.

[5] Arber III. 88.

[6] Rymer's *Foedera* xvii. 253, quoted by Ames-Herbert, page 1419.

"for Mr Leggatt's Rent 5s." In 1599, "For buriall of a Child "wh. died at Mr Leggatt's." In 1609, he was elected Churchwarden[1].

Leonard Greene in a document already alluded to[2], says that Legate hired a house in the Regent Walk for his printing-office; and as Greene lived in St Mary's parish from 1612, he must have been in a position to have accurate information on the subject. Could this be the shop for which Legate paid rent 5s. to the parish?

11. JOHN PORTER.

On 17 June 1593, John Porter and John Legate prosecuted John Tidder in the Vice-Chancellor's court for offering books for sale in the Cambridge market[3]. I can find no record of Porter's appointment, but he lived in Cambridge[4], and was evidently one of the stationers appointed by the University at this time. He was a member of the Stationers' Company, and is probably the John Porter of Haslyngfylde who was apprenticed to Cutbert in 1568 (Arber, *Stat. Reg.* I. 375). Some of Perkins's books are printed for him (in 1595, etc.) with John Legate, and Walsall's Sermon in 1607 'for I. Porter and Len: Greene of Cambridge.'

12. CANTRELL LEGGE.

Cantrell Legge was apprenticed to his predecessor John Legate, as appears from the following entry:

1589: 26 April. Cantrell Legge sonne of Edwarde Legge of Burcham in the Countie of Norffolk Y[e]oman, hathe put himself apprentize to John Legat Citizen and Stacioner of London for Eighte yeres from midsomer nexte [24 June 1589] ij' vj'ᵈ solutum gardiano .6. maij[5].

[1] " Also Mr Legatt, and Walter Betson were chosen churchwardens for the yere and have payd for their dismission for a fine cyther of them x'. to thuse of the said parish." Parish Book Great St Mary's, 1609.
[2] Registry MS. 33. 1. 11. [3] Registry MS. 33. 2. 1.
[4] See Appendix C. [5] Arber, *Stat. Reg.* II. 157.

Legge was sworn and admitted freeman of the Stationers' Company, 11 December 1599[1]. He was appointed printer to the University by Grace, 5 June 1606. He is said to have been in partnership with Legate, but their names never appear together, and Legate's name never appears as Legge's agent in London for the books printed at Cambridge, which would have been but natural had any partnership existed. From the date of Legge's appointment entries of books under his name occur very frequently in the Stationers' Registers, and in nearly all cases in connection with some of the London Stationers—Leonard Greene, Thomas Man, &c.—showing the kind of partnership that still to a small extent exists in what are known as "Trade editions."

With the growth of the Cambridge press the difficulties with the Stationers' Company seem to have increased, for in 1620 Legge petitioned the Lords in Council on a prosecution by the company for printing Lilly's *Grammar*[2]. On 29 November 1623 the Privy Council made an order defining the rights of the University[3]. But this evidently did not satisfy the Stationers, as in 1624 the company complained that

About two yeares since one legg, printer of Cambridge, printed great nombers of Psalmes, and endeauored to iustifie the Doing thereof, by Colour of some generall wordes in a Charter made by King Henry the VIIJ[th] to that vniuersity...The said Legg being assisted by the vice Chancellor, and some Doctors proceeded in printing the *psalmes* to the great hindrance of the Companie of Staconers and almost to their vtter vndoing[4].

The complaint also extends to the printing of Almanacks. In the year 1623 there was a grace of the Senate to examine the orders concerning the printers. Legge died in or before 1629, as on June 1 of that year his widow transfers her interest in 16 books of her late husband to Boler[5].

[1] Arber, *Stat. Reg.* II. 724. [2] See Appendix B.
[3] Cooper's *Ann.* III. 161- 2. [4] Arber, *Stat. Reg.* IV. 527.
[5] Arber, *Stat. Reg.* III. 212.

Legge appears in the Parish Book of St Mary the Great from 1607 to 1623.

In MS. Coll. Regin. Oxon. CLV. p. 227 is the certificate of Nicholas Hide and Thomas Richardson, Attorney and Solicitor-General, as to the difference between Norton, the King's printer, and Legge, the printer to the University of Cambridge, 1621. (Cooper's *Additions to Annals*, 331).

13. THOMAS BROOKE, M.A., Clare.

The date of Brooke's appointment does not appear; but on 2 June 1614 there was a Grace for granting him a new patent, as he had lost his old one. There is in the Registry (MS. 33. 1. 6.) his resignation dated December 4; but without year. This could not have been before 1621, as in the copy of the MS. 'Foundation of the University of Cambridge' by John Scot written in that year[1], his name still appears as one of the printers.

He probably resigned in the year 1624, in which case Leonard Greene, who was appointed in 1622, would be in place of John Legate, who died in 1620; and Thomas and John Buck appointed in 1625 would take the places of Cantrell Legge and Thomas Brooke. Brooke also held the office of Esquire Bedell; he died in 1629.

14. LEONARD GREENE.

Leonard Greene was a member of the Company of Stationers, having been admitted freeman April 14, 1606[2]; and the first book registered with his name appears in the following month:

John Porter & Leonard Grene. Entred for their copie vnder the handes of Master Pasfield & Master Norton Warden Meditacons Diuine & Morall, a third Centurie [By Bishop Joseph Hall] vj.

[1] See p. 295, *note*.   [2] Arber III. 683.

He was appointed one of the printers to the University by Grace, Oct. 31, 1622[1], and on Dec. 16, 1625, there is a second Grace for sealing a patent to him in conjunction with Thomas and John Buck[2].

How long his connection with the University lasted can only be inferred from a statement of his own. In a document[3] containing charges against his partner, Thomas Buck, he avers that he had a knowledge of books and printing "by reason of his "trade therein for the space of thirtie years almost." If this period included the time of his apprenticeship, it would date from about the year 1599, so that these charges were probably written about the year 1629. In the same document he claims to have sent everything to the Cambridge press, even books that were entirely his own property, and as we find in 1630 a book printed in London "for Leonard Greene of Cambridge," it is probable that his connection with the Cambridge press had ceased by that time. I do not find any entries in Arber's Registers after the year 1629.

The following entries occur in the St Mary's Parish Book. In 1612, Greene appears as paying jointly with W. Williams (described in 1607 as "bookbynder") 'Rent of shops 13s. 4d.' In the following year each name is entered separately for the same property, Leonard Greene "For hys shop at the south side of the steple, 6s. 8d.", while Williams pays a like sum for the shop on the north side. From 1614 to 1617, the two names appear together as paying jointly, and after the latter year the entry ceases. From 1620 to 1629, Greene pays annually a sum

---

[1] The imprint in Crakenthorpe's *De Providentia Dei* (March, 162⅔) is 'Cantabrigiæ, impensis Leonardi Greene unius e Typographis Academiæ.' J.

[2] Accordingly in William Bedell's Latin version of Pietro Sarpi's *History of Italy under Paul V.* (the dedication of which is dated March 28, 1626), we find Thomas and John Buck and Leonard Greene appearing together on the title-page as University Printers. J.

[3] This is the document (Registry MS. 33. 1. 11) already alluded to, p. 294 and p. 296, and quoted on p. 300.

of 4s.; in 1623 and 1626, he signs the Churchwardens' accounts
as one of the Auditors; and he would appear to have died in
1630, as in that year there is an entry "for buriall of Mr Leonard
Greene, 6s. 8d."

15. THOMAS BUCK.

Thomas Buck, M.A. and one of the Esquire Bedells, was
appointed by Grace, July 13, 1625. He would appear to have
held the office of printer, or to have retained some interest in it,
for upwards of 40 years, as after the death of John Field in 1668
there is a petition of T. and J. Buck against his estate. During
this time Buck had several partners, none of whom seem to
have found it easy to work with him, and much of the information that we get regarding the press is derived from their complaints and petitions addressed to the University authorities.
The first is Leonard Greene, who was appointed three years before him, and in whose petition we read :

> That whereas L. Gr. beinge acquainted with the matter of bookes and
> printinge by reason of his trade therein for the space of thirtie yeeres
> almost, and Mr Bucke being unexperienced, haveing lead a students life, the
> said L. Gr. did hide nothinge and conceale nothinge from the said Mr Bucke
> nor spare any paines (although to the hindrance of his owne busines divers
> from this) whereby the common benefite of the presse might be furthered.
>
> That for divers copies the sole printinge whereof the said L. Gr. might
> have had for his owne profite as he is of the Company of Stationers of
> London, he hath ever brought to this presse, notwithstandinge he hath
> but a third part therein (and some of them and the best were his before
> ever Mr Bucke came into the place), and besides the charge of printinge at
> Cambridge is decrer then at London[1].

Greene then proceeds to complain of Buck taking as a new
printing-office in his own name, and without consulting him,
the Angell[2], "leased from Mr Lukyns," Greene desiring instead

---

[1] Registry MS. 33. 1. 11.
[2] Called at different times St Mary's Hostel, New Inn, and Angel. It
stood, as I am informed by Mr J. W. Clark, on the site now occupied by
the Senate House and the portion of Senate House Passage between that

"that the presse might be placed in a house most convenient
"for all their coming to it, as the Regent walke (in all men's
"opinion the fittest), which Thomas and Legatt had successivelie
"all their time hired—or els at the house where Mr Craine
"dwelt[1]."

Thomas Buck's next partner was his brother John, also one
of the Esquire Bedells, who was appointed by Grace Dec. 16,
1625, and who probably printed in partnership with him[2] from
that time, although I find no record of any partnership arrangement. As early as 1627, we find the names of T. and J. Buck
alone together on the title-page of a poem by Phineas Fletcher[3].
On May 15, 1632, articles of agreement were drawn up between
T. and J. Buck, by which John assigned his printing patent to
Thomas for seven years for a payment of £56 a year, and agreed
to execute his brother's duties as Bedell during this period. Within two years of this agreement, differences arose between the two
brothers, and copies of documents relating to these differences
are in the Registry (MS. 33. 1. 21). The two brothers however retained a joint interest in the press to a much later period,
as they appear together as claimants against John Field's estate
in 1668.

Roger Daniel was appointed by Grace July 24, 1632, and
articles of agreement were entered into between him and Thomas
Buck, Aug. 21–22 following. From MS. 33. 1. 19, we learn that

building and Caius College. In the Audit book, 1695, there is an entry
"To the Bursar of Bennet College a years rent for the ten' called St
Mary's Hostel, now part of the New Inn due Mich. 1695 £1 4 0." This
site however would seem to be as central as the Regent walk itself.

[1] There is a note in the St Mary's Parish Book by the late Mr Thomas
Stevenson to the effect that Mr Craine's house was that in which he was
then (1837) living. The house (at the corner of Trinity and St Mary's
Streets) is that now occupied by Macmillan and Bowes, and before Stevenson's time was occupied by Nicholson, commonly called ' Maps.'

[2] See note on p. 299.

[3] *Locustæ vel Pietas Jesuitica*, etc. by Phineas Fletcher. Cambridge,
1627. 4to. J.

Daniel agreed to take

That Capitall messuage and tenement called the Augustine Fryars[1]
wherein the said Thomas Buck now dwelleth together with the printyng
house & all other houses yards orchards closes wayes & all other ease-
ments & commodities thereunto belonging,

for a period of six years at the rate of £190 a year paid quarterly, this sum to include the two patents of Thomas Buck and
John Buck.

On Feb. 2, 1633, new articles of agreement[2] were entered
into for five years, by which Thomas Buck was to receive two-
thirds of the profits and Roger Daniel one-third. On March 14,
1634, or in less than two years from the first agreement, Daniel
complains[3]: "that whereas the petitioner was about August last
"was twelve month chosen to be one of the University printers"...he had been led by Buck to enter upon conditions that he
was not able to fulfil, and he asks the University to allow him
to print independently of Buck. In a document[4] written at the
same time as the petition from which the foregoing extracts are
taken, he represents to the University the advantage that would
arise from the establishment of more than one printing house.

That parting of the printers will beget in them a laudable emulation
which of them shall deserve best either in the books set forth, or the
manner of their setting forth, or the materialls.

It would appear therefore that although the University continued the old practice of appointing three printers, only one office
existed up to this date. Notwithstanding these complaints, the
partnership between T. Buck and Daniel did not come to an
end, as their names occur together for several years, and on
Sept. 5, 1639, articles of agreement were entered into between
Buck and Daniel on the one part and certain London stationers
on the other. The press was in a condition of great activity
during the period that Buck was connected with it. There was

---

[1] The site of the New Museums in Pembroke Street and Free School Lane.
[2] MS. 33. 1. 20.   [3] MS. 33. 1. 22.   [4] MS. 33. 1. 23.

an agreement with Edward Weaver[1], a London stationer, for three years to supply 500 reams of Almanacks; while not less than nine editions of the Bible were printed between 1628 and 1640.

From 1640 to 1650, Buck's name does not occur on the title-pages of books[2], but only Daniel's. In the latter year, however, Daniel's patent was withdrawn, and in 1651 and 1652, Buck's name again appears as 'printer to the University.' He is said to have resigned in 1653, but I cannot discover the authority for this statement, and as has already been seen, he claimed some interest in the business in 1668, only two years before his death in 1670.

Buck was elected Fellow of Catharine Hall, March 16, 161⅚, being then B.A. He took an active part in College affairs, especially in acquiring land for the new building, and " out of " the love and affection which he beareth to our said College " advanced money out of his own pocket for this purpose, as appears by entries in the College books between 1622 and 1637. In 1622, he was " M.A. and Fellow "; Jan. 27, 162¾, "Fellow and " late Steward"; 1624, "one of the Esquire Bedells"; 1630, (Jan. 7) he is described as "late Fellow". Between 1624 and 1630, only two Fellows were elected, viz. July 9, 1627 and Jan. 7, 1630, and one of these must have been in the place of Buck. The Rev. G. F. Browne (who has kindly made the extracts from the College books from which the above facts are taken) inclines to the later date.

In 1632, Buck was living[3] at the house called the 'Augustine Friars,' which is in the parish of St Edward, and as his name is in the parish book of St Edward's in 1667 and 1669, it is probable that he continued to live there till the time of his death.

---

[1] MS. 33. 1. 12, 13.

[2] In 1640, Gerard's *Meditations* is printed by Roger Daniel for Thomas Buck. J.

[3] See p. 302.

16. JOHN BUCK.

John Buck, one of the Esquire Bedells, was appointed printer by Grace, Dec. 16, 1625, and seems to have been living in
1668. Such particulars as are known respecting his connexion
with the Press will be found under Thomas Buck. He was
married and lived in the Parish of St Botolph. A son, Samuel,
was baptised Nov. 18, 1632. Another son, John, was baptised
June 11, 1635, and buried June 4, 1636. In 1669 "Mrs Bucke,
John Bucke's wife was buried." In 1660, there is an entry of
£5 received from Mr John Buck given by Mr Brooks for the
poor of St Botolph Parish.

17. FRANCIS BUCK.

Francis Buck was appointed printer by Grace, Oct. 27, 1630,
and resigned July 21, 1632, so that he held the office for less
than two years. His name does not occur in any of the agree-
ments between Thomas Buck and his various partners, nor have
I ever seen it on the title-page of any book.

18. ROGER DANIEL.

Daniel was appointed by Grace July 24, 1632, and it has
been necessary to give the main facts of his connection with
the Cambridge press in a preceding section—that on Thomas
Buck. I cannot find his name among those who were admitted
freemen of the Stationers' Company up to the year 1640. In
the year 1638 I find on the title-page of a large Bible Printed
at Cambridge by Buck and Daniel "and are to be Sold by
"Roger Daniel, at the Angell in Lumber Street, London." His
name occurs on title-pages at a later date at the Angell, and it
is therefore clear that while acting as one of the printers to

the University, he had a book shop, perhaps also a printing office, in London.

On 23 August, 1642, the House of Commons ordered

That Roger Daniell, Printer to the University of Cambridge, be forthwith summoned to attend the House, concerning printing the Book set forth in Defence of the Commission of Array[1].

And on September 3 it was ordered

That Mr Daniel, the Printer of the University of Cambridge, be injoined by this House, not to print anything concerning the Proceedings of Parliament, without the Consent or Order of one or both Houses of Parliament: And that he be discharged of further Attendance[2].

In January $164\frac{2}{3}$ the House of Commons took offence at the publication of *The Resolving of Conscience*, etc., by Henry Fern, D.D., afterwards Bishop of Chester. Roger Daniel was taken into custody of the Serjeant at Arms for printing this work; but on the 2nd of February the House ordered him to be forthwith bailed, and on the production of the warrant for the printing under the hand of Dr Holdsworth, the Vice-Chancellor, it was

Resolved, upon the Question, that Dr Holdsworth forthwith be sent up, in safe Custody, at his own charges: and that Captain Cromwell be desired to take care to send him up accordingly[3].

Daniel's patent was cancelled for neglect on June 1, 1650, but he continued to print books in London; for instance, in 1651[4], his shop is "in vico vulgò dicto Pater-noster-row, aulâ vero Lovelliana," and in 1658 he appears as the printer of a book 'at the Angel'.

[1] *His Majesties answer to the Declaration of both Houses of Parliament, Concerning the Commission of Array: Of the first of July* 1642. Printed by his Majesties speciall command, At Cambridge, By Roger Daniel, Printer to the famous Universitie. 1642. 4to.

[2] *Commons' Journals*, II. 733, 751 quoted in Cooper *Ann*. III. 332.

[3] *Commons' Journals*, II. 900, 951, quoted in Cooper *Ann*. III. 337.

[4] See the titlepage of *Patriarchae siec Iesu Christi Genealogia per Mundi aetates traducta a D. Emmanuele Thesauro*. 1651. 8º. J.

19. JOHN LEGATE (THE YOUNGER).

John Legate, the younger, was admitted freeman of the Stationers' Company 6 September, 1619, and in the following year entered[1] certain publications of his father, 42 books in all, 26 of them being by Perkins. He is said by Ames to have obtained in 1626 licence to print Thomas's *Dictionary*, and he continued to use the University stamp and to describe himself on the title-pages of books[2] as Printer to the University, as his father had done, although I can find no reference to any appointment till 1650. It seems probable therefore that until this year he traded on his father's name. He was appointed one of the University printers by Grace July 5, 1650, evidently in succession to Roger Daniel, whose patent was cancelled on June 1 of the same year. On October 10, 1655, Legate's own patent was cancelled for neglect.

In a list [without date: about 1635] of "The names of suche as keepe printing-houses" there is the following entry:

Master John Legate succeeded John Legate his ffather about 14 yeeres since, I beleeve never admitted, but as I have beene credibly informed his ffather being Printer for Cambridge, and there printing some of the [Stationers'] Companies privileged Ware, to their prejudice; was by the Company allowed to set up and worke here on condicon he would doe so no more (he hath no other right) (he hath sold away his printing house at Cambridg[e])[3].

In the Register of St Botolph Parish there is the following entry:

1642.   John Leggat and Elizabeth Grime married June 25.

---

[1] Arber IV. 45.

[2] e.g. in 1626, 1628, 1633, 1648.

[3] Arber, *Stat. Reg.* III. 701 from *State Papers* Charles I. vol. 307. Art. 86. The sentences printed within brackets are added subsequently.

20. JOHN FIELD.

John Field was appointed printer by Grace Oct. 12, 1655. Before that date he was "printer to the parliament," in which capacity he produced many editions of the Bible, that of 1653 in 32mo. forming the subject of an article in Disraeli's *Curiosities of Literature*, "Pearl Bibles, and 6000 errata." His name occurs on the title-page of Bibles as early as 1648 and as late as 1668, the year of his death. He would seem to have continued his London press, at least for a time, after the date of his appointment as printer at Cambridge, as books were printed by him in 1658, in which he describes himself as "one of His Highness's Printers." In a pamphlet entitled *The London Printers Lamentacon, or, the Press opprest, and ouerprest*, there is a fierce attack on Field and the two other Republican printers, Newcome and Hills:

Who printed the pretended Act of the Commons of England *for the setting up an High Court of Justice, for the tryall of his Martyred Majesty* in 1648? Or, *the Acts for abolishing King-Ship, and renouncing the Royall Line and Title of the Stuarts? Or, for the Declaring what Offences should be adjudged Treason? For taking the Engagement? for sale of Dean and Chapters Lands? for sale of the Kings, Queens and Princes Goods and Lands; and the Fee-farme Rents? for sale of Delinquents Lands;* or, *the Proclamation of* 13. *of September* 1652 after the fight at Worcester, *offering, One Thousand pound to any person, to bring in his Majesties person?* but only John Field Printer to the Parliament of England (and since by Cromwell was and is continued printer to the University of Cambridge!)...Have they [Hills and Field] not invaded and still do intrude upon His Maiesties Royall Priviledge, Prærogative and Præeminence; and by the pusillanimous Cowardize and insignificant Compact of Master Christopher Barker [the younger], and another of his name, and (not without probable suspicion) by the consent and connivance of Master John Bill (though he was artificially defeated in his expectations of profit;) Have they not obtained, (and now keep in their actuall possession) the Manuscript Copy of the last Translation of the holy Bible in English (attested with the hands of the Venerable and learned Translators in King James his time) ever since 6 March 1655?[1]

[1] Arber, *Stat. Reg.* III. 27, 28.

There is a letter dated August 17, 1668, from Charles II. to
the Vice-Chancellor, desiring that a printer be not yet appointed in succession to the late John Field, whose estate is
considerably engaged in the service of the press. Field appears
in the St Botolph Parish Books as paying rates from 1657 to
1668. He held office in 1660 as Churchwarden and Headbrow[1].
Field built in 1655 a new Printing Office in Silver Street
(Carter 469), the University having for that purpose taken a
lease of the ground from Queens' College for a term of years;
and by several renewals this continued to be the University
printing-office till about 1827, when the Pitt Press was commenced. It stood on the north side of Silver Street, on a
portion of the site now occupied by the new Master's Lodge of
St Catharine's College.

21. MATTHEW WHINN, M.A., ST JOHN'S.

The Grace for sealing Whinn's patent is dated 16 March
1669. He also held the office of Registrary, to which he was
elected in 1645.

22. JOHN HAYES.

John Hayes was appointed printer by Grace Oct. 14, 1669,
it having been decided by the Heads of houses on July 7 to
lease the printing to him for £100 a year, the office having
been left open for nearly a year in consequence of the letter of
Charles II. of August 17, 1668, already alluded to under John
Field. There is in the Registry a bond (dated 28 October,

---

[1] Head-borough, Head-borrow. In England formerly the chief of a
frank-pledge, tithing, or decennary, consisting of ten families. Called in
some counties Bors-holder, that is, Borough's elder, and sometimes tithing-
man. In England Head-boroughs are now known by the name of Petty-
constables. *Imperial Dictionary* (Ogilvie and Annandale, 1883).

1703), by which J. Hayes and J. Collyer undertake to pay £150 a year to the University so long as Hayes continues Printer[1]. He seems to have done so until the following year, and from a tablet in Botolph Church we find that he died 28 November 1705, aged 71. In the year 1696 active measures were taken to improve the condition of the press. The Duke of Somerset, Chancellor, wrote to the Vice-Chancellor on June 29 of that year suggesting the re-establishment of the press; stating that £800 had been raised towards the erection of a new building, and offering to endeavour to raise a further like sum. In this work however Hayes would appear to have had no part, as in all arrangements for the purchase of new type, &c., his successor, Cornelius Crownfield, who was then acting as Inspector of the Press, seems to have been always employed.

From the time of Field, 1655, the University Printing Office has continued in the Parish of St Botolph[2], and the printers therefore appear as ratepayers, &c., in that parish. Hayes so appears from 1669 to 1705; in 1672 he was elected sidesman and in 1669 churchwarden.

23. JOHN PECK, M.A., ST JOHN'S.

The Grace for sealing his Patent is dated 20 October 1680. He also held the office of Esquire Bedell, to which he was elected in 1669.

---

[1] Registry MS. 33. 1. 32.

[2] Samuel Sewall, the American judge, describes it in 1689. 'By it [Katherine Hall] the Printing Room, which is about 60 foot long and 20 foot broad. Six Presses. Had my cousin Hull and my name printed there. Paper windows, and a pleasant garden along one side between Katherine Hall and that. Had there a Print of the Combinations.' *England in* 1689. *Being extracts from a Diary etc.* Communicated to the Massachusetts Historical Society, Boston, U.S.A., 1878, by James Greenstreet: Printed for the Society, 1878, and reprinted in *Walford's Antiquarian* for September, 1885, page 129.

24. HUGH MARTIN, M.A., PEMB.

The Grace for sealing his Patent is dated 9 December 1682. He received a salary of £5, but in the year 1691 there is a Grace for an augmentation by consent of the Heads for three years, and during that and the two following years there is an extra payment of £5 to him and to Jonathan Pindar. On October 10, 1698, there is a Grace for an annuity of £5 each to Martin and Pindar, "formerly elected printers." Martin received that salary certainly till 1705, and probably till 1716. He also held the office of Esquire Bedell from 1680 to 1716.

25. DR JAMES JACKSON.

The Grace for sealing his Patent is dated 7 November 1683.

26. JONATHAN PINDAR[1].

The Grace for sealing his Patent is dated 11 June 1686.

27. H. JENKES.

Grace for sealing Patent 30 March 1693. He received a salary of £5, with an extra £5 "by consent of the Heads." In 1698 there is in the Audit Book Mr Halman for Mr Jenkes 1 year and a ½ as printer, £7. 10s.; more, an additional gift to Mr Jenkes "as he is a poor man", £7. 10s.

[1] The name of Pindar occurs frequently in the University Books and Parish Registers. A Jonathan Pindar appears in the St Mary's Parish Book in 1625. From the Audit Books we learn that in 1656-7 Jonathan Pindar received £5 "in consideration of his paines in the Library in transcribing several Catalogues"; and in 1692, 1693, 1694 payments were made to a bookbinder of the name. In 1693 there is a payment "To Goodwife Pindar by order of the Audit £3."

28. JONATHAN PINDAR.

The Grace for sealing his Patent is dated 8 September 1697. Like his namesake, he received as printer a salary of £5, with additions. On August 28, 1730, there is a Grace declaring the voidance of the office of Printer to be necessary before certain proposals for printing Bibles and Prayer-Books can be settled, and offering Pindar the continuance of his full salary after his resignation.

29. CORNELIUS CROWNFIELD.

The nomination and pricking for election of Crownfield took place December 16, 1705, and the Grace for sealing his patent is of date Feb. 11, 170$\frac{5}{6}$[1]. But although his formal appointment did not take place until this date, he was engaged in the service of the press for many years before the death of John Hayes, and would seem to have been the business adviser of the Curators of the press from 1698, the year in which they were first appointed[2].

There exists among the documents at the Press the Minute-book of the Curators from 1698 to 1741, which affords much information about the work then going on, and from which copious extracts have been made in Mr Chr. Wordsworth's *University Studies*, Appendix IX. At the meeting of the Curators on August 23, 1698 (which appears to have been the first), leave is given to Mr Tonson, of London, to print 4to. editions of Virgil, Horace, Terence, Catullus, Tibullus, and Pro-

---

[1] After the revolution, one Cornelius Crownfield, a Dutchman, who had been a soldier, and a very ingenious man, had that office, as he told me himself in Cambridge in 1739, and is since succeeded by Mr Joseph Bentham. Ames (1749) p. 462.

[2] Grace January 21, 169$\frac{7}{8}$. Among the Curators is "Mr Laughton, Coll : Trin : Academiae Architypographus."

pertius; and on the same day it was agreed that Cornelius
Crownfield have leave to send to Rotterdam for 300 lbs. of
double pica for printing the same. On Nov. 9, 1698, it was
resolved that Mr Crownfield be allowed ten shillings per week
for the inspection of the press. In the minutes of March 1,
169⅚, an order is directed to be signed by "the Delegates and
Mr Crownfield the Printer."

The University now for the first time undertook to manage
the Press for itself. Hitherto the University had appointed
the printers in the first instance, but had left them to make
the business arrangements at their own risk, and print what
they chose, so long as it obtained the *imprimatur* of the University authorities. Henceforward every book printed was
sanctioned directly by the Curators, who determined the price
per sheet, and among other details appointed some competent
person to correct for the press.

The minutes consist largely of permissions to Cambridge
booksellers to print books at the press; the names of these
booksellers, Webster, Jeffery, etc., are found on the title-pages.
Among them frequently appears the name of Crownfield himself, from which it would seem that he was a bookseller on
his own account, as well as being University printer. An
agreement with Tonson of London is mentioned above; one
book at least is printed for a Newcastle bookseller. On
October 4, 1701[1], they entered into an agreement with John
Owen of Oxford Stationer for the production of an edition of
Suidas' Lexicon, 3 vols. folio; Owen to pay £1. 10s. 6d. per
sheet, paying for the first 100 copies when the second 100
were ready for delivery, and so on, six months credit being
given for the last 200. The whole stock was to remain
at the Press as security till paid for. Owen evidently was
unable to fulfil his part of the engagement, as on April 16,
1703, a Grace was passed for a new contract with Sir T. Jannson,

[1] Registry MS. 33. 6. 31; Minutes of the Curators. p. 18.

in place of John Owen, insolvent. Owen's failure placed the
University in difficulties with regard to the work, and correspondence and negotiations respecting it went on for a period
of 40 years. Owen had one large book printed in Cambridge in
1703—the first volume of Cellarius' Geography. The second
volume was printed at Amsterdam in 1706.

On Feb. 25, 17$\frac{39}{40}$, a resolution was passed to appoint a new
inspector, and to allow the present, now infirm, to continue his
full salary; and on March 24, 1740, it was resolved that Joseph
Bentham be appointed in the room of C. Crownfield.

Crownfield was living in the parish of St Edward from 1700
to 1704, as, with other parishioners, he signs the parish book
at the Easter meeting in each of those years. He may have
been living there before 1700, but there is no list of parishioners
given in the book. From 1707 he appears in the rate book of
St Botolph. In that year there is an entry of a 22 months' rate
"Cornelius Crownfield for the Univ. £1. 13s. 0d.," the first time
it appears in this form, and probably the first time that the
rate was paid directly by the University, as Hayes paid a fixed
sum to the University for his printing rights, and so would pay
rate on his own account. In 1726 the rent on which Crownfield
is rated is £16, and his name continues till 1742. In the
registers there are entries of baptisms and burials of several
children: 1710, James baptized; 1710, Anne-Penelope, baptised; 1711, Catern buried; 1714, Thomas, baptized[1]. In 1733
is an entry "Mary, wife of Cornelius Crownfield, buried" and
Nov. 4, 1743, Cornelius Crownfield, printer to the University.

In St Botolph Book, March 1, 1715, is the following entry:

Received of Mr Crownfield for the year 1708 seven shillings for a piece

[1] There were two of the name of Crownfield who graduated at Clare:
Henry, entered July 9, 1715, pupil of Mr Laughton; Thomas, entered
May 27, 1729, pupil of Dr Wilcox, afterwards Fellow of Queens'. The
latter would not improbably be the son of Cornelius Crownfield.

of ground commonly called the round O in his garden which should have been paid at 1 shilling the year for the use of the poor.

There was an Adrian Crownfield married and living in the parish at the same time, who is sometimes described as "junior"; and in 1760 the names of C. and J. Crownfield appear on the title-page of a book.

Carter states that from 1696, when Crownfield was appointed Inspector of the Press till 1707 [he should have said 1705], when Hayes died, there were two printing offices: one that then in use [1753 when Carter wrote] and where Hayes printed; and the other the Anatomy School and Elaboratory. After much search I am unable either to confirm or rebut this statement. In its favour there is the evidence of the Minute Book of the Curators from 1698, in which Crownfield's name frequently appears, but Hayes' not at all. Against there is the fact that Hayes alone appears in the parish book as rate-payer, neither the University nor Crownfield coming in the book till 1707, after Hayes' death; and Crownfield having lived certainly till 1704 in the parish of St Edward. The following entries from the University audit book show that payments for printing were being made both to Hayes and to Crownfield during the period in question:

		£	s.	d.
1697.	Mr Hayes the Printer, a Bill	25	3	0
1698.	,, ,, ,,	5	13	6
	A book of Verses, Mr Hayes, for Printing	40	0	0
1702.	Mr Hayes for 15 Psalm Books and printing the Assize of Bread	0	12	6
1702.	Mr Crownfield for printing combinations &c. this year and paper for the same	2	10	0
	Verses: Crownfield for paper £6 12s. and £16	22	12	0
	Paid Press account for printing 31 sheets	16	14	0
	Mr Hayes for printing Hebrew, &c. Verses	2	0	0
1703.	,, ,, ,, the Assize of Bread	5	11	0
1704.	,, ,, ,, ,, ,, ,, ,,	0	15	0
1705.	Mr Crownfield's Bill for Combination Verses, &c.	5	14	0

30. W. FENNER, MRS FENNER, AND THOMAS AND JOHN JAMES.

It will be more convenient to deal with these four names together. On December 29, 1730, the Syndics resolved to lease the right of printing Bibles and Prayer-Books to James and Fenner; and on April 23, 1731, a lease was granted to W. Fenner for 11 years. This license was granted to Fenner for the special purpose of printing from stereotype plates. In Nichols' *Literary Anecdotes*, Vol. II. 721 will be found a full account of this matter, from which we quote :

William Ged, an ingenious artist, was a Goldsmith in Edinburgh, and made his improvement in the art of printing in 1725 * * * * In July 1729 William Ged entered into partnership with William Fenner, a London stationer, who was to have half the profits, in consideration of his advancing all the money requisite. To supply this Mr John James, then an Architect at Greenwich,......was taken into the scheme, and afterwards his brother, Mr Thomas James, a Founder, and James Ged, the inventor's son. In 1730 these partners applied to the University of Cambridge for permission to print Bibles and Prayer-Books by Blocks instead of single types, and, in consequence, a lease was sealed to them April 23, 1731. In their attempt they sank a large sum of money, and finished only two Prayer-Books : so that it was forced to be relinquished, and the lease was given up in 1738.

It will be seen that the first attempt to work from stereotype plates was made at Cambridge, and that it was not at that time successful. Fenner died insolvent about the year 1734, and his widow continued the printing under the lease, not-withstanding the strong protests of John James, who claimed that *he* had got the concession from the University, that he and his brother Thomas had found about £1000 of the capital for which they had had no return, and that Fenner's name was inserted in the lease only because he was a practical printer, while his partners were not. There was a long correspondence between John James and the University, in which he charged the Fenners with dishonesty towards him ; and to these charges

Mrs Fenner replied. The matter was only settled in 1738, by a composition, and Mrs Fenner relinquishing the lease.

Certain London Stationers, with Baskett, King's Printer, entered June 28, 1732, a Bill in Chancery against Fenner for printing Bibles, but on August 4, 1733, an order was obtained to dissolve the injunction against the defendants. Although the action was taken against Fenner, it was really an attack on the printing rights of the University.

Thomas and John James were the sons of a London type founder; Thomas, who was also a type founder, was greatly injured in purse and in health from his connection with Ged's invention, and died in 1738.

At a later period stereotyping was revived by Alexander Tilloch, editor of the *Philosophical Magazine*, who did not know of Ged's plan, and obtained a patent for a similar invention, which he afterwards relinquished. But the exertions of Andrew Wilson were more successful; and an account of his arrangements with the University will be found under the year 1804.

31. JOSEPH BENTHAM.

On Dec. 13, 1740 there was a Grace to appoint a Printer *durante bene placito;* the nomination of Joseph Bentham and W. Goodbed took place the same day; and Joseph Bentham was elected on the next. On January 5, 174½, the suit of Baskett *v.* Bentham was commenced, by which the King's Printer sought to prevent the University Printer from printing an abridgment of the Excise Acts, and the litigation was continued until 1758. On Nov. 24 of that year the Court of King's Bench decided in favour of the University. On Jan. 20, 174¾, there was a Resolution of the Syndics that Mr Bentham is to sell no Bibles without an order from one of the Syndics. On Feb. 26, 1749, the Syndics resolved that Mr Bentham should demand of all Authors in arrear with the Press, the payment of all sums due within twelve months. On Nov. 7, 1765, the Syndics resolved to appoint an assistant to Bentham. John Archdeacon was appointed Inspector of the Press in place of Joseph Bentham, Oct. 29, 1766 and on Dec. 13, Bentham resigned. The Syndics allowed him to retain the use of the house at the Press.

Bentham, one of 10 children, was the son of the Rev. Samuel Bentham, Vicar of Witchford near Ely, and descended from a very ancient family in Yorkshire, and brother of James Bentham the historian of Ely Cathedral. He was an Alderman of the town, and died June 1, 1778, aged 68, and was buried in Trumpington Church.

Bentham appears as ratepayer in the Parish of St Botolph from 1743 to 1779. On March 2, 174$\frac{3}{6}$ the rental on which rating is made is £22, but other properties are added in subsequent years. 1761, New Printing Office, £12, and Tenements, Silver Street, £5. 5s. and £2. 10s., Pembroke Lane £2. 5s., Black Lion Yard £4, Cock Yard £2. 10s. From 1767 New Printing Office £12 is rated to Archdeacon (in 1771 it is described as "White Lyon Warehouse"): from same date he pays £11, part of Printing Office. From 1779 Archdeacon pays the whole.

32. JOHN BASKERVILLE.

John Baskerville, the celebrated type founder and printer of Birmingham, was born at Wolverley in the County of Worcester in 1706; in 1726 he became a writing master at Birmingham; in 1737 taught at a School in the Bull Ring; in 1745 took a large building to carry on the business of a Japanner; and in 1750 tried his first experiments in type founding, in which business and that of printer, he was chiefly engaged for the next 15 years. He was elected printer for 10 years from December 16, 1758, according to Articles of Agreement dated December 15. The

following letter written to the Vice-Chancellor in May of the
next year will show what work he was engaged upon.

Birmingham, 31 May, 1759.

Sir,

I have at last sent everything requisite to begin the Prayer Book
at Cambridge. The Bearer M'. Tho. Warren is my Deputy in conducting
the whole. I have ordered him to inform you of every step he takes,
and to desire you would appoint a person to tell out the number of sheets
before they go to press and again before they are packed up for Birmingham. M'. Bentham will inform you how many sheets per 1000 are
allowed for wast. I have attempted several ornaments, but none of them
please me so well as the specimen; which I hope will be approved by
you and the Gentlemen of the Syndick. I propose printing off 2000 the
first impression, but only 1000 of the State holidays &c. which the
patentee has left out. The paper is very good and stands me in 27/ or
28 the ream.

I am taking great pains in order to produce a striking title page and
specimen of the Bible, which I hope will be ready in about six weeks.
The importance of the work demands all my attention; not only for my
own (eternal) reputation; but (I hope) also to convince the world, that
the University in the honour done me has not intirely misplaced their
Favours.

You will please to accept, and give my most respectful duty to the
University, particularly to the Gentlemen of the Syndick. I should be
very happy if I could make an Interest to a few gent° to whom the work
would not be disagreeable, to survey the sheets, after my people had
corrected them as accurately as they are able that I might, if possible
be free from every error of the press; for which I would gladly make
suitable acknowledgment. I procured a Sealed copy of the Common
Prayer with much trouble and expense from the Cathedral of Litchfield,
but found it the most inaccurate and ill printed book I ever saw: so that
I returned it with thanks.

I am S' Y' most obed' hble Serv'
JOHN BASKERVILLE.

Addressed on the back

The Rev'd Doctor Caryll Vice Chancellor
of the University of
Cambridge.

In a letter to Horace Walpole dated Easy Hill, Birmingham,
Nov. 2, 1762 he thus speaks of his arrangements with the
University:

The University of Cambridge have given me a grant to print their 8vo. and 12mo. Common Prayer Books: but under such Shackles as greatly hurt me. I pay them for the former, twenty, and for the latter twelve shillings the thousand; and to the Stationers' Company thirty-two pounds for their permission to print one edition of the Psalms in metre to the small Prayer-Book; add to this the great expense of double and treble carriage; and the inconvenience of a double printing-house an hundred miles off. All this summer I have had nothing to print at home. My Folio Bible is pretty far advanced at Cambridge which will cost me 2000l all hired at 5 per cent. If this does not sell, I shall be obliged to sacrifice a small patrimony, which brings me in 74l a year, to this business of printing, which I am heartily tired of, and repent I ever attempted. It is surely a particular hardship, that I should not get bread in my own country (and it is too late to go abroad) after having acquired the reputation of excelling in the most useful art known to mankind; while every one who excels as a Player, Fiddler, Dancer, &c. not only lives in affluence, but has it in their power to save a fortune[1].

On July 3, 1761, articles of agreement were entered into between the University and Baskerville, and they are probably those alluded to in the foregoing letter. He produced his folio Bible in 1763, and Nichols says that after that he seemed to have become weary of his printing, and that in 1765 he wrote to his friend Dr Franklin, then in Paris, to see if he could dispose of his types. Franklin answered, "that the French, reduced by the "War of 1756, were so far from being able to pursue schemes of "taste, that they were unable to repair their public buildings, "and suffered the scaffolding to rot before them." He died in 1775.

33. JOHN ARCHDEACON.

John Archdeacon, a native of Ireland, was appointed Inspector of the Press in place of J. Bentham, Oct. 29, 1766; the latter having resigned December 13 following, Archdeacon was elected Printer December 15. On May 26, 1768, a resolution of the Syndics of the Press fixed his salary at £140 per ann., without any contingent advantages. Although Archdeacon's

[1] Nichols *Lit. Anecd.* vi. 453 n.

appointment as Inspector was not made until 1766, it will
presently appear that he was connected with the Press in
the previous year. In Nichols *Lit. Anec.* Vol. II. 459, we
read :

> In consequence of overtures from a few respectable friends at Cam-
> bridge, Mr Bowyer had some inclination towards the latter end of 1765,
> to have undertaken the management of the University Press, by purchasing
> a lease and their exclusive privileges, by which for several years they had
> cleared a considerable sum. To accomplish this he took a journey to
> Cambridge ; and afterwards sent the compiler of these anecdotes to
> negotiate with the Vice-Chancellor. The treaty was fruitless ; but he
> did not much regret the disappointment.

Nichols wrote to Bowyer as follows :—

> Sunday afternoon Sept. 15, 1765.
>
> Good Sir
> I write to you now from the house of Mr Labutt, with whom I have
> dined, and who has most obligingly shown me all in his power. Mr Arch-
> deacon is not at home. I have opened to Mr Labutt my plan, who is of
> opinion that something may be done. I have talked also with a com-
> positor, who is sensible, and who now works in the house. Six hundred
> a year I believe may carry it. They *talk* of *ten* having been offered. For
> 7 years last past the University have *cleared one-thousand-three-hundred
> pounds* annually ; besides farming the Almanack (200l more). This might
> at least be *doubled by opening the trade* in new channels. If any book-
> seller of reputation would enter into a scheme with you, an *immense
> fortune would certainly be raised*.......

In Bowyer's reply he says :

> Mr Archdeacon as you observe, must be a leading person, and there
> is some delicacy necessary to be shown to him.

A note is added :

> Mr John Archdeacon, a very excellent printer ; whom the University
> appointed to succeed Mr Bentham ; and who continued in that office
> several years. He died at Hemingford Abbots, Sept. 10, 1795, æt 70.

The following is extracted from a letter of the Rev. William
Ludlam of St John's College[1]:

> For my own part, I am sometimes forced to make types, which are
> commonly brass, of which I here send you a specimen (‡a ǂb ±c).

[1] Nichols *Lit. Anecd.* Vol. VIII. 414.

It is called plus-minus ±. I printed my first tracts at Cambridge, when Archdeacon (not Bentham) was their printer. I was very sick of it ; the University meanly provided with mathematical types, insomuch that they used daggers turned sideways for *plus's*. They were sunk into arrant traders, even to printing hand-bills, quack-bills, &c., which they then for the first time permitted for Archdeacon's profit. As to table-work of which I had a deal, they knew nothing of it ; and many a brass rule was I forced to make myself....... I complained of this to Mr Bowyer, and would have had him print my essay on Hadley's quadrant; but he was too full of more important work. I remember I told him I had marked all Archdeacon's damaged letters ; which were not a few, especially in the italic. To which the old gentleman replied "I dont like you the better for that."

Archdeacon did not die till 1795, but his successor, John Burges, was appointed in 1793, and from that date until the death of the former, the two names appeared together as printers.

Archdeacon first appears in the books of St. Botolph, rated at £5, Sept. 1759; at £6, 3rd Quarter 1761; June 23, 1767, £12 for New Printing house (in 1771, described as "White Lyon Warehouse"); Dec. 3, 1771, £11 (half of the printing office, Bentham paying the other half); March 15, 1779, the remaining half of printing office, £11. This total, £34, continued till the end of Archdeacon's residence at the Press, 1794. He died[1] at Hemingford Abbots, Sept. 10, 1795, age 70.

34. John Burges.

John Burges was elected July 1, 1793, and, until Archdeacon's death in 1795, acted in partnership with him. He died April 16, 1802, aged 54, and was buried in St Botolph's Church. He appears in the rate book of St Botolph from July 4, 1794, to July 7, 1802, paying, like Archdeacon, on a rental of £34. The name of John Burges is in the books of the parish from Sept. 23, 1776, for a house in Pembroke Lane, formerly held by Archdeacon, rent £2. 5s. This may have been the same John Burges who was afterwards printer.

[1] Nichols' *Lit. Anec.* Vol. II. 460 n.

35. JOHN DEIGHTON.

John Deighton was elected April 28, 1802, received his patent July 28, and resigned December 11 in the same year. Although he only held the office of printer for about eight months, he was apparently connected with the press, even at that time, as publisher. On 5 July, 1803, a bond was executed by J. Deighton, F. Hodson, and R. Newcome, for securing payment of £2323. 10s., the price of the whole of the University stock of 8vo. Bibles (MS. 33. 1. 44).

A volume with four catalogues of J. Deighton, belonging to Messrs Deighton, Bell and Co., which has been kindly lent to me by Mr W. W. Smith, contains at the end the following entries :

J. Deighton commenced Book-binder at C	May 1.	1777
Bookseller at C	Jan. 1.	1778
Married	Feb. 11.	1779
Removed to London	Jan.	1786

A later hand has added in pencil :

Qy returned to Cambridge, Feb. 1795, successor to Merrill.]

The first " Catalogue of Books, including the Library of the " Rev. Dr Barnardiston, late Principal Librarian to the University "of Cambridge, and Master of Corpus Christi College," is· dated November, 1778, and Deighton describes himself as successor to Mr Matthews, bookseller, near Great St Mary's Church. At the end of the catalogue he is called Book and Printseller, Stationer and Bookbinder, but the word " Print " is drawn through with the pen, and " near Great St Mary's Church" is changed in the same way to " opposite the Senate House." In the three other catalogues, dated Dec. 4, 1780, Nov. 1783, and Dec. 1784, the address is given as opposite the Senate House, so it is not improbable that, before he went to London, Deighton's shop was on the site of that occupied as a bookshop

successively by the second John Nicholson, son of "Old Maps,"
from 1807, by Thomas Stevenson from 1822 ; and by Macmillans
since 1846.

John Deighton would appear to have returned to Cambridge
in 1795, and, perhaps, as suggested above, to take the business
of J. and J. Merrill, one of the most important in Cambridge
during the last half of the 18th century. His two sons, John
and Joseph Jonathan. were in partnership with him from 1813,
and he died in the parish of St Michael, 16 January, 1828, aged
80. From 1827 the two sons carried on the business as J. &
J. J. Deighton till 31 Aug. 1848, when the latter died, aged 56,
and was buried in St Bene't churchyard. From that date John
Deighton continued the business alone till 13 July, 1854, when
he died at the age of 63, and was buried in Grantchester
churchyard. After his death the business was bought by
Messrs George Bell and W. W. Smith, and has been carried on
since then under its present style of Deighton, Bell and Co.

36. RICHARD WATTS.

Richard Watts was elected Dec. 16, 1802, and his connection
with the Press terminated by his resignation in 1809. From
1802 to June, 1806, the rate in the St Botolph books is entered
as for University Printing Office ; from Sept. 1806 to Dec. 1809
in the name of Richard Watts. The rent is still £34. From a
pamphlet entitled "Facts and Observations relative to the state
"of the University Press," printed towards the end of 1809, it
would appear that serious differences had arisen between the
Syndics and Watts. In the spring, 1808, two of the Syndics—
Dr Milner and Mr Wood—were appointed to investigate the
Press accounts, and they requested Mr Watts to make out a
statement of the accounts for the five years, Michaelmas, 1802
to Michaelmas, 1807. The Syndics represented that, whereas
during the 15 or 20 years prior to 1802 there had been a profit

of not less than £1500 a year; under Watts' management for the five years ending 1807 there had been no profit at all. Watts, irritated by the enquiry, resigned June 13, 1808, and at the next meeting of the Syndics his resignation was accepted. A subsequent application to withdraw his resignation "in con-"sequence of the more due consideration of the causes which "led to it," was made to the Syndics, but they resolved that no answer could be given till the examination of the accounts was concluded, and apparently the matter was never re-opened. The accounts were not finally completed till June, 1809, when Mr Watts, having surrendered his patent into the hands of the Vice-Chancellor, it was resolved that a new printer be elected in October. In his final letter of June 17, 1809, Watts admits certain mistakes in the accounts, and that the pecuniary result was not what might have been expected. After leaving Cambridge Watts went in the first instance to Broxbourne, where his name appears in the parish books from 1810 to Nov. 1815. In the latter year there appeared an octavo edition of Walton's *Angler*, with imprint: " London : printed for Samuel Bagster, in "the Strand, by R. Watts, at Broxbourne, on the River Lea, "Herts., 1815." About the end of 1815[1] he left Broxbourne, for London ; and early in the following year a book printed for the Church Missionary Society has imprint: "Printed by "Richard Watts, Crown Court, Temple Bar, London," with date "Lady-day, 1816." While at Broxbourne he was appointed Printer to the Hon. East India Company's College at Hailey-bury, and retained the appointment after his removal to London, printing for the College Classical and Oriental Examination Papers for Professor Jeremie and others. He paid special attention to printing, in Oriental and other Foreign

---

[1] For the information respecting Watts after he left Broxbourne I am indebted to Mr C. Cornish, of Messrs Gilbert and Rivington, Limited ; and for the examination of the Broxbourne Parish Registers to Mr J. S. Vaizey, Barrister-at-Law, Churchwarden.

languages, Bibles, Testaments, and other works for the British and Foreign Bible Society, Church Missionary Society, &c. He printed also Monier Williams' *Sanskrit Dictionary*, Johnson's *Persian Dictionary*, Wilson's *Glossary of Indian Terms*, and some of the Catalogues of Oriental Books and MSS. in the British Museum.

He died at Edmonton, March 24, 1844, at an advanced age, and was succeeded by his son, William Mavor Watts, who, in 1867, the premises being required for the new Law Courts, removed to Gray's Inn Road. On March 19, 1870, a fire destroyed the premises with all the types. Fortunately the punches and matrices were preserved in another building, and Mr Watts retiring from business on account of ill-health, these passed into the hands of Messrs Gilbert and Rivington, who re-cast the types and added many others.

37. ANDREW WILSON.

Early in 1804, and soon after Richard Watts had been elected printer, a proposal was made to the University by Andrew Wilson, a London printer, that he should on terms to be agreed upon communicate his secret respecting stereotyping. This secret was the invention of Earl Stanhope, who refused to receive anything in respect of it, or even the repayment of a sum of £6000 spent in experiments. In what it differed from the invention of Ged in 1725, which was exercised in Cambridge by Fenner and James 1730—38, does not appear; and as Ged's invention was not a pecuniary success it is possible that it was forgotten, and that Lord Stanhope's invention was entirely independent of it. Dr William Chambers, writing in 1867 says, that the art of stereotyping has undergone little change since its invention by Ged.

A preliminary agreement was drawn up between the Syndics and Wilson, April 20, 1804, under which Wilson was to receive for a period of fourteen years one-third of the savings effected by stereotyping; and jointly with Watts the University Printer to act as agent for the sale of the Bibles and Prayer Books. To estimate the savings, each party was to appoint an arbitrator, and these in case of difference had power to appoint an umpire. The work of stereotyping under this preliminary agreement had not been going on for two years before the services of the arbitrators were required, and in 1806 Wilson's Case was printed in a pamphlet of 44 pages. The nature of the agreement would be very likely to lead to differences, unless the items that were to form the basis of the calculations of savings were clearly defined. In Wilson's 'Case' he claims that the stereotype process having enabled the Syndics, by an expenditure of £1500, to turn their warehouse into a printing-office instead of building a new one at a cost of £4500, the difference, £3000, was a stereotype saving in which he had a right to participate.

On March 6, 1807, an agreement between the Syndics and Wilson provided for the payment of a bill for stereotyping plates amounting to £865. 16s. 9d., on condition that some of the plates not then delivered should be delivered within one week; and that Wilson within eight weeks should make and deliver the plates for a nonpareil Welsh Testament, charged at the same rate as those contained in the bill. It was further provided that the University should make so many stereotype plates of 8vo. editions of Ainsworth's Dictionary and Johnson's Dictionary as should come to the amount of Wilson's bills, he supplying at once the original types for the purpose; and a bond for £2000, with R. Watts as surety, was executed to secure the payment of one-third of the amount, and of £500 advanced for the purchase of types, on the delivery of the plates and return of the types; one-third in nine, and one-third in eighteen months. It was a condition that this agreement should bind neither party in other matters in dispute. The following are the details of Wilson's bill:

EXAMPLE 1.

	£.	s.	d.

The Bourgeois Testament in Mr Wilson's Bill July 10, 1805 :

Casework of 228 pages at 2s. 4d. per page   26 12 0

Reading ¼th 6 13 0

Double of the above two sums 66 10 0

Alterations, over-running, &c. £11. 1s. 10½ : the double of this 22 3 9

One set of plates 470 lbs. 4 oz. at 3s. per lb.. viz. the price per lb. of Bourgeois types 70 10 9

£159 4 6

A printer's principal gain being upon the press-work, one half of the sum thus arising exclusive of the alterations (viz. £137. 0s. 9d.) is added to allow a sufficient profit ; proceed therefore thus : brought forward . . . 159 4 6

Allowance instead of press-work 68 10 4½

A second set of plates half price, exclusive of alterations, over-running, &c. 68 10 4½

£296 5 3

EXAMPLE 2.

Mr Wilson's bill for 126 pages of the Brevier   £. s. d.
Testament, August 31, 1805, casework and reading at 1s. 8d. and 5d. per page   13 2 6

The double of this sum £26 5 0

Plates 1st set, 155 lbs. 9 oz. at 3s. 6d. per lb.
the price of Brevier types . . . 27 4 6

Allowance instead of press-work . . . 26 14 9

A second set of plates 26 14 9   £106 19 0

EXAMPLE 3.

Mr Wilson's bill for the Welsh Test. May 7, 1806 :

Casework and reading 14 sheets at £5 . . 70 0 0

The double of this £140 0 0

Alterations, over-running &c. £17. 4s.
The double of this 34 8 0

332 plates containing 428 lbs. 8 oz. at 3s. 6d.
per lb. the price of the types . . . 74 2 3

£248 10 3

Allowance instead of press-work . . . 107 1 1½

A second set of plates 107 1 1½   462 12 6

£865 16 9

August 8, 1807. An agreement was entered into for the acquisition by the University of Wilson's stereotype secret, for which the following sums were to be paid:

£2000 on execution of the agreement.

£1000 advanced to Wilson, May 29, 1805, to become his property.

£1000 when the sales from March 25, 1807, shall exceed £4500 : £2 for every £45 of such excess till it reaches £1000 ; but if that sum shall not be reached till March 25, 1818, no further payment to be made[1].

In 1811 a case was submitted by the University for the opinion of Sergt. Lens and Mr Leycester. It is stated that the Syndics consider the charge made by Wilson for stereotype plates was unreasonable, and that in agreeing to pay the amount of £865. 16s. 9d. they expected to get a corresponding advantage to themselves in supplying the plates of Ainsworth and Johnson on the same principle[2]. Wilson refused to send the types from which to set up these books till he was informed how many plates he would have for the sum. During the four years since the agreement was made, wages had largely increased, and counsel held that they were by the agreement bound by the prices of 1807. It is probable that the work was never done, but there is nothing to show how the arrangement with Wilson ended.

There is a hypothetical case, not dated, but placed among the papers of 1811 (33. 7. 28) of which the following is a copy :

Whether supposing A. B. to be acquainted with the secret mode of making stereotype plates, and supposing C. D. to know the mode now in general use, and whereas it is conceived that the secret is now no secret. Supposing A. B. to inquire of C. D. his (C. D's) mode of making the plates, and by his answers it appeared that he (C. D.) was acquainted with all the peculiarities of the secret, would A. B. be justified in telling C. D. that such was the secret ?

38. John Smith.

John Smith was elected Nov. 11, 1809. On Nov. 2, 1836, a Grace was passed allowing him a pension of £200 a year

---

[1] Registry MS. 33. 7. 26.   [2] Registry MS. 33. 1. 27.

(half his salary), after a long period of service as printer. He died at Thetford, Norfolk, August 16, 1840, and there is a tablet in St Botolph's Church, in which parish he was born Sept. 12, 1777.

From the St Botolph books it appears that Smith, as University Printer, was rated at £34 (Printing Office £22, and Warehouse £12) till April 16, 1827. For the following quarter, July 12, 1827, he is assessed at £45 for printing office and house. Oct. 7, 1830, there is in addition, old premises, £11, and this ceases July 11, 1831, being erased from the book after having been entered. Oct. 21, 1831, a new entry appears, University late A. Watford, £4. 10s.; Jan. 12, 1832, house and University Press, £45; but now it is placed in Mill Lane and Laundress Lane, instead of Silver Street; and there appears, in Trumpington Street, Univ. late Thos. Hill, £8; late Mrs Hill, £5; late Wm. Neal, £10; late John Glasscock, £8. 5s.; late James Nutter, £24; late Thos. Eddlestone, £7; late Wm. White, £10; late A. Watford, £9. 10s. July, 1832, Pitt Press sites of houses, £94. 5s.; Oct. 3, 1833, house, J. Smith, in Mill Lane, £10; in addition to printing office, £45, Silver Street, Univ. warehouse, £15; Univ. old office and house, £23. April 14, 1836, old office, £23, ceases. University Press property:

	£.	s.	d.
Pitt Press, Trumpington Street . . .	94	5	0
University Warehouse (Silver Street) . .	15	0	0
John Smith's house, Mill Lane . . .	10	0	0
University Office and Warehouse . .	45	0	0

39. JOHN WILLIAM PARKER[1].

John William Parker was elected Nov. 15, 1836, and held office till 1854. But his connection with the Press dated from an earlier period. In the year 1828, the Press having been

[1] For much of the information respecting Parker I am indebted to an article in the *Bookseller*, June 1, 1870.

found to be in an unsatisfactory condition, the Syndics con-
sulted two eminent London printers—Mr Clowes and Mr
Hansard—on the subject. At the request of the University
that the former would come to Cambridge and examine the
Press, he sent his overseer, Mr Parker; and in February, 1829,
on Mr Clowes being appointed superintendent of the Press at a
salary of £200 per annum, he accepted the office, performing
his duties through Mr Parker. The latter was able very soon
to justify the selection of the Syndics, and to make the Press a
source of profit. One of the first things he did was to turn to
account some of the old and apparently useless stereotype
plates, and in this he was most successful. He was soon
able greatly to increase the accounts with the Bible Society
and with the Christian Knowledge Society, and in other
ways opened up channels of trade for the disposal of University books. Upon the resignation of John Smith in 1836
he was appointed printer, with a salary of £400 a year,
he visiting Cambridge for two days once a fortnight. After
much opposition he succeeded in introducing steam power, but
for many years the Bible Society resolutely set their faces
against the purchase of books so printed. An amusing illus-
tration is given in the *Bookseller*, June 1, 1870.

Some idea may be formed of the amount of reduction in
prices of Bibles and Prayer-Books, during the time of Parker's
management, from the Report of the University Commission of
1852:

	1830.		1850.	
	s.	d.	s.	d.
Price of Cheapest Bible . . .	2	5	1	10
„ Medium Bible . . .	7	2½	3	7½
„ Cheapest Prayer Book .	0	6½	0	2¾
„ Medium Prayer Book .	1	7¼	1	3

The Commissioners remark on this reduction in prices:

Much of this great reduction of price is attributable to improved
machinery and to better arrangements in the establishment; much of it

is more apparent than real, arising from the inferiority in paper and execution; the rest from a reduction of profits, which, in the case of the Cambridge Press, has not been compensated, as has been usual in similar cases, by a very great increase in production. On the contrary, the number of Bibles and Prayer-Books produced has rapidly diminished.

The Commissioners attribute these results partly to the "virtual abolition of the monopoly" by which the profits were reduced to the "ordinary commercial standard, and in some "respects even below it (for private subscriptions were brought "in aid of the production of cheap Bibles in Scotland)."

Parker, whose father had been in the Navy, was born about the year 1792; was apprenticed to Mr Clowes, and stayed with him till 1832, when he left to commence business as a publisher at 445, West Strand. He was appointed "publisher of "the books issued under the direction of the Committee of "General Literature and Education appointed by the Society "for Promoting Christian Knowledge." The publishing business soon became an important one, and Parker's catalogue ultimately contained the works of Whately, Whewell, Hare, Trench, Maurice, Kingsley, Froude, Helps, Miss Yonge, G. H. Lewes, Buckle, &c. &c.; and a large proportion of the educational books produced at Cambridge. In 1843 his son, John William Parker, jun., came into the business. On his death in 1860 Mr Parker took his old assistant, Mr William Butler Bourn, into partnership; but in 1863[1] the business was sold to Messrs Longmans, and the house of Parker, Son and Bourn ceased to exist. Mr Parker resigned his office of Printer in 1854 and died May 18, 1870, aged 78.

---

[1] *Fraser's Magazine* for October, 1863, was published by Parker, Son & Bourn: the number for November by Longman & Co.

40. {CHARLES JOHN CLAY, M.A., Trinity.
41. {GEORGE SEELEY.
42. JOHN CLAY, M.A., St John's.

The Cambridge University Commissioners of 1850–52, in
their Report, published in 1852, about two years before the resignation of John William Parker, gave it as their opinion that

> It is only by associating printers or publishers in some species of
> co-partnership with the University, or by leasing the Press to them, that
> any considerable return can hereafter be expected from the capital which
> has been invested in it......we are satisfied that no Syndicate, however
> active and well chosen, can replace the intelligent and vigilant superin-
> tendence of those whose fortune in life is dependent upon its success.
> (Report, pp. 136-7).

This opinion was at variance with that of the Syndics of
1850, as given in the same volume (*Evidence*, p. 21). But very
shortly after the issue of this Report it became necessary,
on the resignation of Mr Parker, to appoint a new printer;
and the Syndics, in their Report May 26, 1854, recommended
a partnership with Mr George Seeley and Mr C. J. Clay.
This recommendation was carried out in July. Mr Seeley re-
tired in 1856; a new partnership was entered into with Mr Clay
alone, and that continued until 1882, when Mr John Clay, son
of Mr C. J. Clay, was also admitted as a partner.

In the Report of 1852 we find the following particulars:

> The office contains frames, fittings and appurtenances for 70 com-
> positors; presses and appurtenances for 56 press-men; eight printing
> machines, which require about 50 men and boys to manage, work and
> supply them. A ten-horse steam-engine; two boilers; turning-lathe,
> forge and circular saw, occupying at present, four hands; one (steam-
> power) milling machine, hydraulic and screw hot-presses, at which,
> together, 100 men and boys might be employed if necessary.

The great increase in the prosperity of the Press, since
the above was written, 32 years since, has entirely confirmed
the opinion of the Commissioners as quoted above.

It is curious to compare the present condition of the Press with that of 300 years ago, when by decree of the Star Chamber, in 1584, each of the Universities was limited to one press and one apprentice—at the most!

APPENDIX A (see pages 287, 289).

EARLY CAMBRIDGE BINDINGS.

IT is on general grounds quite likely that binding as well as printing went on in John Siberch's shop under the sign of the *Arma Regia*, and that the bindings executed there should bear some identifying mark. The opportunities of examining bindings of that date are however few and far between; I can only refer to one specimen, and that has unfortunately been renovated, so that possibly some evidence has been destroyed.

There is in Lincoln Cathedral Library a volume (T. 4. 3) which contains, among other books belonging to the years 1516 to 1520, *Richardi Croci Britanni introductiones in Rudimenta graeca*. 1520. 4º. It is printed, according to the colophon, "Coloniæ in ædibus Eucharii Cervicorni, anno a Christo nato M.D.XX. mense Maio expensis providi viri domini Joannis Lair de Siborch." But it must have been bound in England; for stamped on the leather are the several badges of the then king of England. The entire ornamentation is formed by three lengths of a roulette pattern side by side within a plain rectangle. The roulette consists of four compartments; the uppermost contains a crowned pomegranate, the next a crowned portcullis, the third a crowned rose, and the lowest a crown over three fleurs-de-lys, with the initials J. S. at the foot, on either side of the lowest fleur-de-lys.

Ames (*Typographical Antiquities*, p. 456) noticed the name
Johannes lair de Siborch in this book, and considered the
type similar to that used by Siberch at Cambridge. The
binding of this copy seems to afford an additional argument
for considering the two varying appellations to belong to one
and the same person.

[There are also specimens of binding, in Cambridge libraries
and elsewhere, which Mr Bradshaw has for some time supposed
to be the work of one or other of the stationers appointed in
1534. Books tooled with a rather large roulette pattern containing fabulous animals and the initials G. G. may be referred
with great probability to Garrett Godfray; and in the case
of Nicholas Speryng the identification seems almost certain.
There exist many octavo volumes in stamped calf, having on
the obverse[1] cover the Annunciation with a 4-mark and the
initials N. S. at the foot, all surrounded by the text ECCE
ANCILLA DOMINI FIAT MICHI SECUNDUM VERBUM TUUM, and
on the reverse cover (above the same mark and initials) St
Nicholas and the three children, with the legend NICOLAUS
SPIERNICK at top and bottom, and a scroll with acorns and
cockatrices (?) at the sides. As a specimen may be named a
Sarum Missal (Paris, Hopyl for Birckman, 1515, 8°) in the
Bodleian (Gough 2); and a pair of covers are among the spoils
of the Douce Collection. A book from Hengwrt (now in my
possession) similarly bound was printed at Paris in 1508. It
would be interesting to obtain a list of all such books that are
now in existence. J.]

---

[1] It seems convenient to borrow these terms from the language of
numismatics, denoting by *obcerse* the front cover, and by *reverse* the other.

APPENDIX B (see page 297).

Extract from the accounts of Dr Mawe, V. C., illustrating the dispute between the University and the Stationers :

Univ. Accounts 1621—22. fol. 261 b.

	£.	s.	d.
Item payed to Mr Tabor for a iourney to London wth Cantrell Legg about the printinge businesse when he was sent for by ye Bp. of Exeter	6	18	4
Item layed out by Mr Tabor when the Vice Chancellor, Dr Warde, Dr Beale, and Legg went to Royston to deliuer a Letter, and Petition to the King in ye behalf of ye Vniuersitye	5	9	6

fol. 262.

Item for a iourney to London Januar. 3 when I went to finish my own businesse, wch I left vnfinished before Christmas, being hastened home to stopp the stationers proccedinge by Petition to the King at Royston	7	1	3

fol. 262 b.

Item spent in a iourney to London by my selfe, Mr Tabor, and Cantrell Legg when the cause was to be heard, betweene the stationers of London and the Vniuersity Printer by the fowre Committies appointed by the King vt patet per diversas billas 28 dayes	33	5	11
Item spent at Newmarket when I went to procure the Kinges leave to sell the Grammars vpon the L{de} certificate .	0	11	4
Item given to the Mr of request to drawe vp the Kinges order for the sellinge of Grammars	5	0	0

1622—23. fol. 267 b.

Item to Mr Tabor for expenses at London when hee went vpp with Cantrell Legg beinge sent for by Warrant from the Counsayle there attendinge with him 9 dayes . . .	13	14	0

APPENDIX C (see page 296).

I. In *A note of all such persons as are privileged by the University of Cambridge and dwelling within the Town of Cambridge*, written between June 5, 1592 (the date of John Palmer's appointment as Archdeacon of Ely) and 1594 (when Duckett was appointed University Librarian in place of John

Matthew so described in the list), the names of the following
stationers are given :

		Assessed at
Mr Watson	. . . .	ii s
Mr Legate	. . . .	xii d
John Porter	. . . .	viii d
Hughe Burwell	. . . . . .	vi d
Manasses Vautrolier	. . . . .	vi d
John Joanes	. . . .	iiii d
Beniamin Prime	. . . . . .	ii d
William Scarlett	. . . . . .	ii d
Jo. Cuthbert	. . . .	viii d
Thomas Bradshawe	. . . . .	viii d

The list, consisting of one sheet (4 pages) folio, is in ·the
Library of Downing College (Bowtell MSS.).

II.   It seems desirable to add here for comparison the
names of stationers which appear in another list of *The privileged persons in the University of Cambridge which are
recorded in the Register's Office*, dated during the year 1624.

> Thomas Mooden [Morden].
> Anthony Harrison.
> Leonard Greene.
> William Williams.
> Phillip Scarlett
> Peter Scarlett.
> Henry Wray.
> Simon Robuck.
> Richard Ewlam.
> Edmund Porter.
> Jonathan Pinder.
> Samuel Disher.
> John Jones.
> Daniel Boyse.
> Richard Ireland.

besides

> Cantrell Legg, Printer.

The list, consisting of two sheets (8 pages) folio, is in the
Library of Downing College (Bowtell MSS.).

APPENDIX D.

Ornaments, Initial Letters and Devices.

It is often convenient, in examining the works of a particular printer, to be able to refer to specimens of the ornaments, &c. which he used to embellish his books. I have accordingly made a collection of some of those which occur in Cambridge-printed books, more complete in the case of the earlier printers, but, as far as I could make it, fairly representative of the whole series.

The books from which the illustrations are taken are as follows :

Augustini *de miseria vitae.* 1521. 4°. Nos. 4, 5.
Galeni *de temperamentis.* 1521. 4°. Nos. 1, 2, 8—13.
Papyrii Gemini Eleatis *Hermathena.* 1522. 4°. Nos. 3, 6, 7.
P. Rami *Dialecticae libri duo.* 1584. 8°. No. 28.
P. Ovidii Nasonis *fabularum interpretatio.* 1584. 8°. Nos. 17, 19, 21, 22.
Jac. Martini *de prima simplicium et concretorum corporum generatione.* 1584. 8°. No. 18.
Harmony of the Confessions of the Faith. 1586. 8°. No. 15.
Whitaker, *Disputatio de sacra Scriptura.* 1588. 4°. Nos. 20, 24, 25, 27.
[1] De l'Espine, *A very excellent discourse,* etc. 1592. 4°. Nos. 14, 16, 23, 26, 34.
Whitaker *adversus T. Stapletoni defensionem.* 1594. F°. Nos. 29, 31, 32.
Perkins *on the Creed.* 1596. 4°. No. 33.
Perkins, *A Reformed Catholick.* 1598. 8°. No. 30.
Heydon, *Defence of Judiciall Astrologie.* 1603. 4°. No. 35.
Epicedium Cantabrigiense. 1612. 4°. Nos. 36, 37.
Davenant, *Expositio epistolae...in Colossenses.* 1630. F°. Nos. 44—47.
Novum Testamentum. 1632. 8°. Nos. 40—42.
Dalechamp, *Christian Hospitalitie.* 1632. 4°. No. 39.
Hausted, *Senile Odium.* 1633. 8°. No. 38, 43.
Garthwaite, *Evangelicall Harmonie.* 1634. 4°. Nos. 48, 49.
Bible. 1638. F°. Nos. 50, 51, 54.

---

[1] Some of the figures were used by more than one printer; in these cases, from whatever book they may have been taken, they are arranged among those of the printer who is observed to have first used them.

Book of Common Prayer. 1638. F°. Nos. 52, 53, 55—61.
Dury, *Summary Discourse.* 1641. 4°. No. 62.
Fern, *Resolving of Conscience.* 1642. 4°. No 63.
His Majesties Declaration, etc. Aug. 12. 1642. 4°. Nos. 64, 65.
Hall's *Poems.* 1646. 8°. No. 86.
Love, *Oratio,* etc. 1660. 4°. Nos. 67, 69.
Kemp, *Sermon,* etc. 1668. 4°. No. 68.
University Queries. 1659 (no printer's name). 4°. No. 70.
Kidd, *Ichabod.* 1663 (no printer's name). 4°. No. 71.
Crashaw, *Poemata.* 1670. 8°. No. 72.
Saywell, *Reformation in England.* 1688. 4°. No. 73.
Barnes, *Edward III.* 1688. F°. No. 74.
Cellarius, *Notitia Orbis Antiquae,* Vol. I. 1703. 4°. Nos. 75, 76, 77.
Bentley's *Horace.* 1711. 4°. No. 78.
Eusebius, *Historia Ecclesiastica.* 3 vols. 1720. F°. Nos. 80, 87.
Middleton, *Bibliotheca Cantabrigiensis.* 1723. 4°. No. 81.
Parne, *Sermon,* etc. 1724. 4°. Nos. 85, 86.
Drake, *Concio,* etc. 1724. 4°. No. 83.
Kerrich, *Sermon,* etc. 1735. 8°. No. 84.
Middleton, *Dissertation on Printing.* 1735. 4°. Nos. 79, 88.
A Collection of Poems. 1733. 8°. Nos. 89—92.
Saunderson's *Algebra.* 1740. 4°. No. 82.
[*Book of Common Prayer.* 1745. F°. See No. 99.]
Gratulatio Acad. Cantabrigiensis. 1748. F°. No. 97.
Mason's *Odes.* 1756. 4°. No. 93.
Advice to a Young Student. 1760 (no printer's name). 8°. Nos. 94, 95.
Gratulatio Acad. Cantabrigiensis. 1761. F°. No. 96.
Lort's *Elegies.* 1776. 4°. No. 98.

So far the illustrations have been taken in facsimile from
the books named. The remainder (Nos. 99—107) are printed
from original woodcuts belonging to the University Press, and
kindly lent by Messrs C. J. Clay and Son. The books given
below are the earliest in which I have noticed the devices
severally named with them.

Book of Common Prayer. 1745. F°. No. 99.
Altar Service. 1814. 4°. No. 100.
Cambridge University Calendar. 1828. 12°. No. 101.
Prolusiones Acad. 1830. 8°. No. 102.
Bible. 1830. Royal 8°. No. 103.
Cambridge Astronomical Observations. 1833. 4°. No. 104.
Irenaeus, Harvey. 1857. 8°. No. 105.
Prayer-Book. 1863. Royal 4°. No. 106.
Pearson *On the Creed.* 1869. 8°. No. 107.

1

2

3

6

4

5

7

8

9

10

11

12

13

14

15

16

17

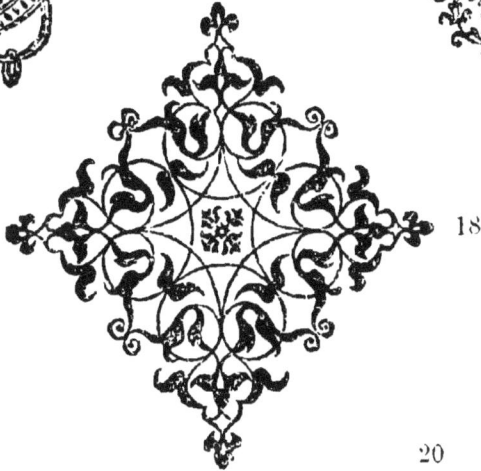

18

20

19

21

23

22

25

24

26

27

28

29

33

34

30

35

31

32

36

37

38

39

43

40

42

41

44

45

46

47

48

49

50

51

54

56

52

55

53

61

60

59

58

57

67

68

69

70

71

The Church of England.

72

73

75

74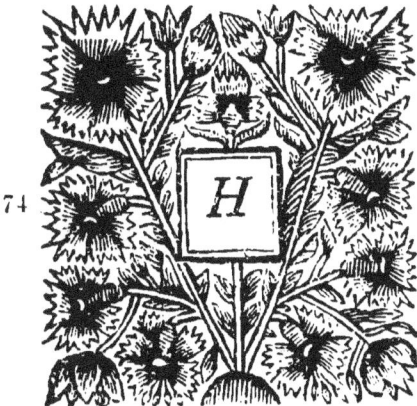

76

ΑΓΝΩΣΤΩ ΘΕΩ

S. Gribelin Sculps:

23

84

85

Lud: Cheron del· NE PRÆSIDIUM & DULCE DECUS *J: Gribelin, sculps:*

86

Lud. Cheron Del: INEC PIETAS NORAM *S. Gribelin sculps:*

87

88

89

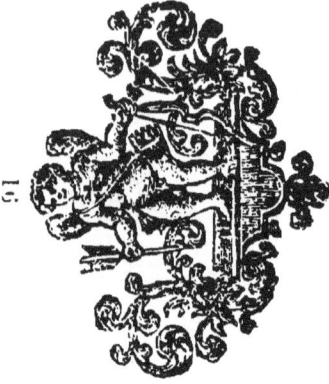

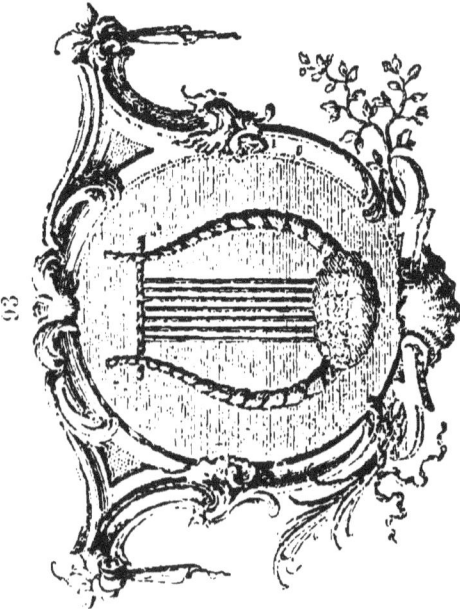

97

98

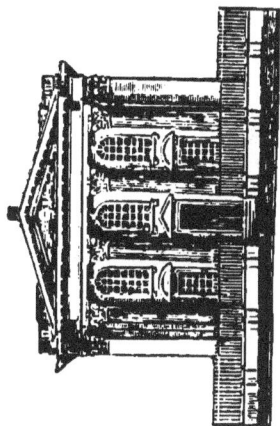

102

103

104

105

106

107

ERRATA.

Page 286, line 16, *omit* John Owen.

On consideration I feel that Owen should not be included in this list, as he does not appear to have been appointed Printer, and his arrangement with the University respecting the edition of Suidas (see pp. 312—13) was purely that of a publisher. His name appears in the first vol. of Cellarius' Geography, 1703 : *Cantabrigiæ, Impensis Ioannis Oweni, Typographi*, with the device No. 77 which does not appear elsewhere ; and again in Simon Ockley's *Introductio ad linguas orientales, Cantabrigiæ: Typis Academicis*, MDCCVI. *Impensis Ioannis Oweni Typographi*. But the denomination 'Typographus' seems to have been used rather loosely.

Page 286, line 30, *for* 1853 *read* 1854.

Page 303, line 11, *for* 1670 *read* 4 March, 16$\frac{69}{70}$.

[From the *Diary* of Alderman Newton, a contemporary of Buck, and living also in the Parish of St Edward. But an entry in St Mary the Great Parish Book, 10 Feb. 1670 (167$\frac{0}{1}$), states that a resolution was passed to sue T. Buck for non-payment of £2 due to the Parish.]

Page 311, Crownfield, par. 2, line 2, *for* 1711 *read* 1749.